UNDERGROUND ANIMAL LIFE

INSIDE AN ARMADILLO'S BURROW

By Rex Ruby

Minneapolis, Minnesota

Credits: Cover and title page, © Ralf Geithe/iStock, © Kuttelvaserova Stuchelova/Shutterstock, © Elena11/Shutterstock, © Christopher Biggs/Shutterstock, and © JasminkaM/Shutterstock; Design elements throughout, © Azure-Dragon/iStock, © marcouliana/iStock, © Nastco/iStock, © GlobalP/iStock, © UroshPetrovic/iStock, © schankz/Shutterstock, and © NP27/Shutterstock, 4, © Ondrej Prosicky/iStock; 5, © Serjio74/Getty Images; 6–7, © Science History Images/Alamy; 8, © Panga Media/Shutterstock; 9, © Matthias Graben/Alamy; 10, © Sandra Kramer / EyeEm/Getty Images; 11, © Dhoxax/Shutterstock, © Lev Kropotov/Shutterstock, and © Heiko Kiera/Shutterstock; 12–13, © klausbalzano/iStock; 15, © Luiz Claudio Marigo/Alamy; 16, © Tierfotoagentur / J. Hutfluss/Alamy; 16–17, © Michael Kurlin/Alamy; 19, © Heidi und Hans-Juergen Koch/Minden Pictures; 20–21, © Ian Fox/Getty Images; and 22, © zelg/iStock, © Scott O'Neill/iStock, © kefkenadasi/iStock, and © tornado98/iStock.

Bearport Publishing Company Product Development Team

President: Jen Jenson; Director of Product Development: Spencer Brinker; Senior Editor: Allison Juda; Editor: Charly Haley; Associate Editor: Naomi Reich; Senior Designer: Colin O'Dea; Associate Designer: Elena Klinkner; Product Development Assistant: Anita Stasson

Library of Congress Cataloging-in-Publication Data

Names: Ruby, Rex, author.
Title: Inside an armadillo's burrow / by Rex Ruby.
Description: Minneapolis, Minnesota : Bearport Publishing Company, [2023] | Series: Underground animal life | Includes bibliographical references and index.
Identifiers: LCCN 2022002359 (print) | LCCN 2022002360 (ebook) | ISBN 9798885091411 (library binding) | ISBN 9798885091480 (paperback) | ISBN 9798885091558 (ebook)
Subjects: LCSH: Armadillos--Juvenile literature. | Armadillos--Behavior--Juvenile literature.
Classification: LCC QL737.E23 R83 2023 (print) | LCC QL737.E23 (ebook) | DDC 599.3/12--dc23/eng/20220120
LC record available at https://lccn.loc.gov/2022002359
LC ebook record available at https://lccn.loc.gov/2022002360

Copyright © 2023 Bearport Publishing Company. All rights reserved. No part of this publication may be reproduced in whole or in part, stored in any retrieval system, or transmitted in any form or by any means, electronic, mechanical, photocopying, recording, or otherwise, without written permission from the publisher.

For more information, write to Bearport Publishing, 5357 Penn Avenue South, Minneapolis, MN 55419. Printed in the United States of America.

Contents

A New Home............................ 4
Amazing Armadillos................ 6
Building a Burrow 8
Day and Night 10
Time for a Treat 12
Staying Safe.......................... 14
A Burrow for Babies............. 16
An Armadillo Pup 18
The Pup Grows Up 20

Be an Armadillo Scientist 22
Glossary................................. 23
Index 24
Read More 24
Learn More Online................. 24
About the Author 24

A New Home

A strange, **scaly** creature crawls out of a hole in the ground. It makes its way into the warm summer evening. The animal is an armadillo, and the hole is its **burrow**. Deep underground, the busy armadillo has been digging a new home!

There are 20 kinds of armadillos. All of them make burrows.

Amazing Armadillos

Each armadillo makes a burrow to fit its size and shape. Adult armadillos can be anywhere from 6 inches (15 cm) to almost 5 feet (1.5 m) long. They live in warm parts of the Americas. Most dig burrows in open **grasslands**, but some of these animals live in forests.

Armadillos are covered in a hard **armor**. This bony layer can be separated into different bands, or pieces.

A band

The smallest kind of armadillo is the pink fairy armadillo.

Building a Burrow

An armadillo begins work on its burrow by digging an **entrance** with the long claws on its front feet. It uses its nose to help break up the soil. Then, it kicks the soil out of the hole with its back feet. The armadillo digs until it has a tunnel that is up to 20 ft. (6 m) long.

Armadillos have four claws on each front foot. There are five claws on each back foot.

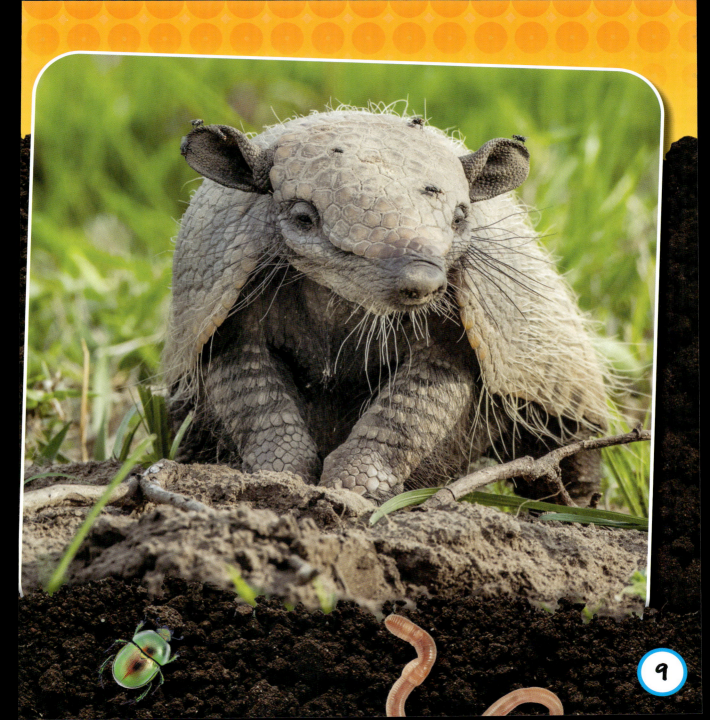

Day and Night

An armadillo may dig many burrows during its life. During the day, it sleeps in a small room at the end of the long underground tunnel. But when evening comes, it wakes up and leaves the burrow. It spends the night looking for food.

An armadillo's cozy bedroom can be up to 5 ft. (1.5 m) underground.

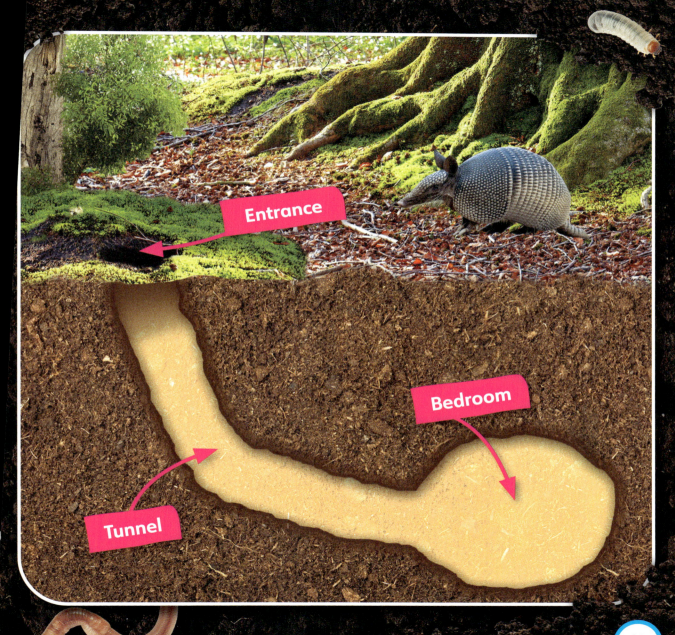

Time for a Treat

What does an armadillo eat? The hungry creature might munch on plants or snack on small animals. But its main food is **insects**. It eats termites and baby insects called grubs. An armadillo doesn't see very well, so it uses its powerful nose to find a feast.

> If an armadillo finds food underground, it uses its nose and claws to dig up the meal.

Staying Safe

An armadillo usually comes out when it is dark outside. But that doesn't always keep it safe. When facing a **threat**, the armadillo tries to hide in its burrow. If it is not near its home, the scared animal might get low to the ground or curl up. One kind of armadillo even surprises **attackers** by jumping into the air.

An armadillo's tough armor protects its body if another animal tries to bite or scratch it.

One kind of armadillo curls up in a ball to stay safe.

A Burrow for Babies

Most adult armadillos live alone. However, they get together to **mate**. Then, soon-to-be-mother armadillos dig new burrows. They make soft nests of grass in the burrows. Mothers give birth to their babies underground.

Armadillos can have anywhere from 1 to 12 babies at a time.

An Armadillo Pup

A **newborn** armadillo, called a pup, looks like a small adult. But the little baby's armor is soft. It will slowly harden as the armadillo gets older. An armadillo pup drinks milk from its mother's body and stays safe in its burrow.

One kind of armadillo always has four pups. They are either all girls or all boys!

Three armadillo pups

The Pup Grows Up

After a few weeks, an armadillo pup begins to spend time aboveground as its mother hunts for food. Soon, it starts to find its own food, too. When it is about six months old, the pup is ready to leave its mother. Then, the first thing the armadillo needs to do is dig a burrow.

An armadillo can live for up to 30 years.

Be an Armadillo Scientist

Some animal scientists look at footprints. Which of these prints do you think were made by an armadillo? What do you think the other prints might be?

Look at the feet of the armadillos in this book to help you decide.

Print A comes from an armadillo's foot. B is a bird's foot. Print C is a cat's foot. And D is a dog's foot.

Glossary

armor a covering that protects the body

attackers things that come at a person or animal with the purpose of causing harm

burrow a hole or tunnel dug by an animal to live in

entrance a place to come in

grasslands dry areas covered with grasses where only a few bushes and trees grow

insects small animals that have six legs, a hard shell, two antennas, and three main body parts

mate to come together in order to have young

newborn a baby that was just born

scaly covered in small pieces of hard skin

threat someone or something that might cause harm

Index

armor 7, 14, 18
claws 8, 12
feet 8, 22
food 10, 12, 20
forests 6
grasslands 6
mate 16
mother 16, 18, 20
nose 8, 12
pups 18–20
size 6
threats 14
tunnels 8, 10–11

Read More

Grodzicki, Jenna. *Armadillo (Library of Awesome Animals)*. Minneapolis: Bearport Publishing Company, 2022.

Riggs, Kate. *Armadillos (Amazing Animals)*. Mankato, MN: The Creative Company, 2023.

Sherman, Jill. *Armadillos (North American Animals)*. Mankato, MN: Amicus, 2019.

Learn More Online

1. Go to **www.factsurfer.com** or scan the QR code below.
2. Enter "**Underground Armadillo**" into the search box.
3. Click on the cover of this book to see a list of websites.

About the Author

Rex Ruby lives in Minnesota with his family. He doesn't live underground, but he would love to explore an armadillo's burrow if he had the chance.